Contents

Exercise is good for you

Your body is like a machine. You need to use it to keep it working well.

Exercise keeps your body strong and fit. You need to be fit to work and play when you want. You should exercise every day to keep fit.

Your heart and lungs are muscles. If you exercise they will work well.

When you use your muscles, they get stronger.

Exercise will make your bones strong.

What About Health?

Exercise

by Fiona Waters

HODDER
Wayland

an imprint of Hodder Children's Books

Titles in the WHAT ABOUT HEALTH? series

Drugs

Exercise

Food

Hygiene

Exercise is a simplified version of the title
Exercise and Your Health in Wayland's 'Health Matters' series.

Language level consultant: Norah Granger
Editor: Belinda Hollyer
Designer: Jane Hawkins

First published in 2001 by Hodder Wayland,
an imprint of Hodder Children's Books.
This paperback edition published in 2003

British Library Cataloguing in Publication Data
Waters, Fiona
Exercise. - (What about health?)
1.Exercise - Juvenile literature
I.Title
613.7'1
ISBN 0 7502 4588 3

Printed in Hong Kong

Hodder Children's Books
A division of Hodder Headline Limited
338 Euston Road, London NW1 3BH

Picture acknowledgements
Illustrations: Jan Sterling
Cover: Hodder Wayland Picture Library; Action Plus 18, 28, 29;
Hodder Wayland Picture Library/(Chris Fairclough) 4, 6, 11, 14 (top), 17, 19, 22, 24, 25, 26; Tony Stone 7, 23; all other photographs Hodder Wayland Picture Library.

Exercise makes you feel and look better.
Exercise helps use up the food you eat.

When you exercise you feel good.

If you choose fruit
and vegetables to
eat, they will help to
keep you fit.▼

Exercise helps you sleep
better. It is like a magic
tonic for your body! ▼

Keeping your body well

Exercise will make your muscles stronger, so you won't get tired when you work and play.

Exercise will make your heart and your lungs stronger, so you won't get out of breath.

Exercise will help you move easily, so you won't feel stiff or sore.

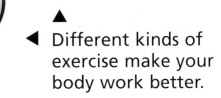

◀ Different kinds of exercise make your body work better.

HOW FAST CAN YOU RUN?

A snail moves at 0.05 km an hour.

We can run at 43.37 km an hour.

A horse can run at 69 km an hour.

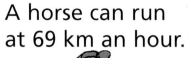

A cheetah can run at 100 km an hour.

If you get out of breath on stairs, you are not fit.▼

If you cannot touch your toes, you are too stiff.▼

▲
If your legs hurt when you are on your bike, your muscles are not strong enough.

Swimming is good exercise for people of all ages. The water holds you up so it is easy to move.▶

Food to make your body work

You need to eat and drink good food to make your body work. If you eat too much, your body will keep all the extra food. Then you will weigh too much. If you do not eat enough you will become tired.

When you are young, you need good food to make your body grow. Your body uses energy all the time, even when you rest.▼

HOW LONG WOULD YOU HAVE TO RUN TO USE UP THE FOOD YOU EAT?

You need to run for more than three hours to use up a burger, large fries and a milk shake.▼

A carrot
5 minutes

An apple
10 minutes

Cornflakes and milk
40 minutes

An egg
20 minutes

A burger and chips
3 hours

Bread, pasta, potatoes and rice will help your body work well. They all turn into energy.

You should eat some of these with every meal. ▶

How to warm up and cool down

When you exercise, you should warm up first. Your body needs to get ready for exercise. You can march or jog on the spot for five to ten minutes. You will begin to feel warm. You will breathe a bit faster too.

When you want to stop, slow down gently first. You will start to breathe more slowly.

Your skin might go red when you are exercising. It is trying to cool you down!

◄ Stretch after exercise, so you don't become stiff and sore.

◀ If you do not warm up first, you might hurt yourself. Your muscles will stretch more easily if they are warm. Try the Blu-Tack test below to see what a difference stretching makes.

Put a piece of Blu-Tack in the fridge. When it is cold take it out. You will find it is hard to stretch. Then warm it in your hands. Now try to pull it.

◀ You should put on warm clothes after you have done any exercise.

Your bones and joints

Your body is made up of lots and lots of bones. These bones are called your skeleton. Your skeleton lets you stand up and walk about.

In some places like your elbow, two bones join up. These places are called joints. Joints help your body move.

Milk helps to make strong bones.▼

Your body makes new bone all the time. Children's bodies make a new skeleton every two years.▼

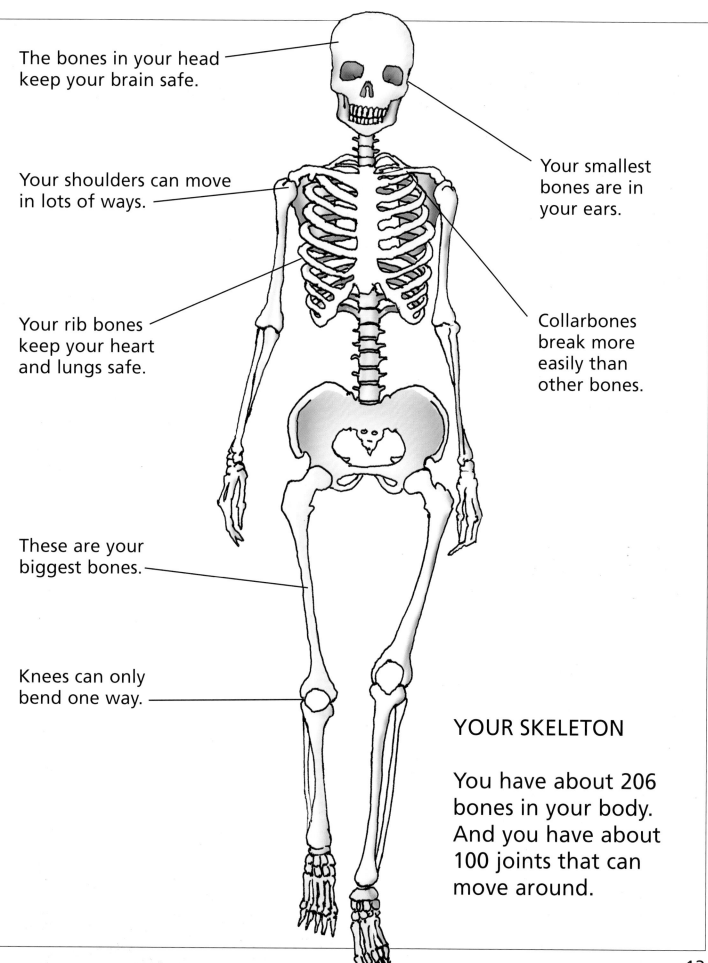

The bones in your head keep your brain safe.

Your shoulders can move in lots of ways.

Your rib bones keep your heart and lungs safe.

These are your biggest bones.

Knees can only bend one way.

Your smallest bones are in your ears.

Collarbones break more easily than other bones.

YOUR SKELETON

You have about 206 bones in your body. And you have about 100 joints that can move around.

Don't get stiff!

If you stretch when you exercise, you will not get stiff. When you are not stiff you can easily bend and twist your body.

If you do not exercise, your joints will get stiff. When you are stiff you can hurt yourself when you do sports.

▲ It is hard to skateboard if you are stiff.

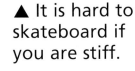

▲ You can't do this if you are stiff!

HERE ARE SOME GOOD EXERCISES TO WARM UP AND COOL DOWN

arm circles

hip circles with your knees bent

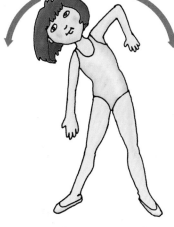

side stretches

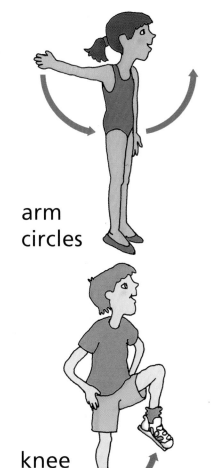

knee lifts

knee bends

Always stretch slowly, and breathe deeply. Hold each stretch for a few seconds.

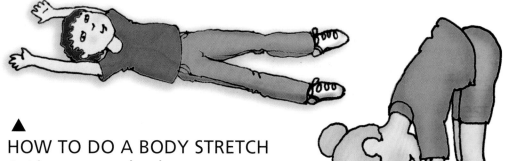

▲

HOW TO DO A BODY STRETCH
1. Lie on your back.
2. Put your arms up.
3. Stretch your legs and your arms.
4. Count to ten.
5. Stop.

◀ Try to touch your toes every day. Soon you will be able to bend further.

How your muscles work

When you walk, your muscles move your bones.
To work, muscles need food and air.
You breathe air into your lungs. Your lungs push the air into your blood. Your blood then carries the air into your muscles.

When you run, your muscles need to work harder. So you need more air. This makes you breathe faster.

Your heart is a muscle. It moves your blood round your body.

Your biggest muscles are in your thighs.

Your smallest muscles are in your ears.

You have more than 600 muscles in your body.
You use 200 muscles to walk.
You use 30 muscles to lift an eyebrow.
You use 15 muscles to smile. ▶

HOW YOUR ARM WORKS:
One muscle gets shorter and pulls your arm up. Then the other muscle gets shorter, and pulls your arm back down. ▶

If all the muscles in your body were able to join together, they could pull five elephants. ▼

If you have been ill in bed your muscles will be weak. You need to exercise to make them strong again. ▼

▲ We all have muscles that can waggle our ears. Can you use those muscles?

Exercises to make you strong

You need to use your muscles to keep them strong. Strong muscles help your joints work well.

If your arms are strong, you can push and pull and lift things. If your legs are strong, you can run and climb and ride a bicycle. Swimming is good for all your muscles.

When you throw the discus your back, arms and shoulders all get stronger. ▶

PUSH-UPS AND LEG-LIFTS MAKE YOUR BODY STRONGER

Push-ups help your arms
and shoulders. ▶

Leg-lifts help
your back and hips.▼

You can exercise your
fingers too! Hold a soft
ball in your hand.
Squeeze it hard. Then let
go. Squeeze it hard.
Then let go. Now use the
other hand. Squeeze it
hard. Then let go.

Your heart and lungs

When you breathe air into your nose and mouth, it goes down a tube. This tube goes into your lungs. Your lungs look like two sacks. When you breathe in, they get bigger. When you breathe out, they get smaller again.

Your lungs push the air into your blood. Your heart moves the blood around your body. The blood then goes into your muscles, to make them work.

Exercise makes your heart and lungs stronger.

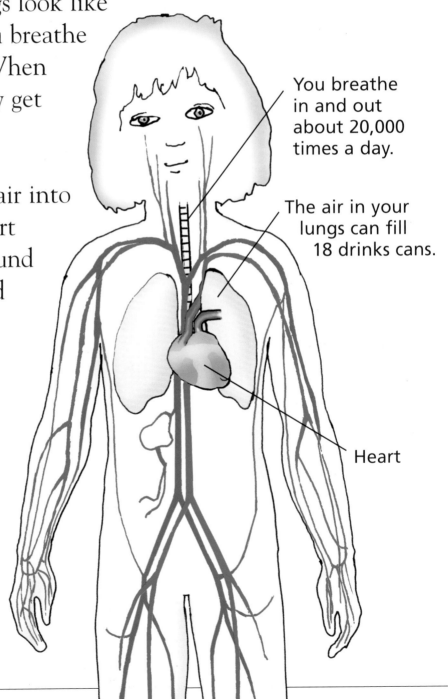

You breathe in and out about 20,000 times a day.

The air in your lungs can fill 18 drinks cans.

Heart

FACTS ABOUT YOUR HEART

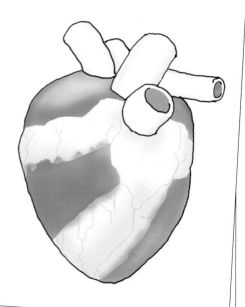

- Your heart beats about 100,000 times a day
- Your heart beats about 70 – 80 times a minute
- An elephant's heart beats 25 times a minute

CHECK YOUR PULSE

Put your fingers on the inside of your wrist. You will feel a beat. This is your pulse. Count how many times it beats in 60 seconds.

Your pulse will beat faster after exercise.

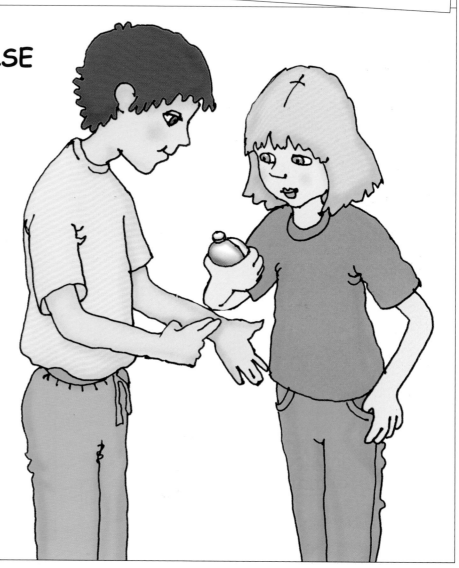

Using air when you exercise

When you exercise, you breathe in lots more air. This helps your muscles to work hard. The more you exercise, the longer you will be able to go without getting tired.

Rollerblading will make your heart and lungs stronger.▼

You need to do about 20 – 30 minutes of exercise three times a week to keep fit.

▲ Stretching exercises are very good for your body.

1. Fill a plastic bottle with water.

2. Put your hand over the top.

3. Turn the bottle upside down in a bowl of water.

4. Get a friend to help you put a tube into the bottle.

5. See how much water you can blow out of the bottle with one big breath.

Look after your body

You should look after your body when you exercise.

Do not exercise just after a meal. Do not exercise if you are ill. Stop if you feel dizzy or sick. If you have asthma or diabetes, ask your doctor what exercise you can do.

You should drink lots of water when you exercise. You need to replace the water you lose when you sweat.▶

CHOOSE THE RIGHT CLOTHES FOR EXERCISE

A tracksuit will help keep you warm.

Wear lots of clothes. Then you can take some of them off as you get hot.

Cotton helps to keep you cool.

Lycra is comfortable.

Wear socks.

Trainers must fit well.

You should wear a helmet and pads if you are skateboarding or rollerblading. ▶

Keep fit!

You should exercise every day. Don't use the lift – walk upstairs instead.

Take care of your body. Don't smoke or take drugs. Eat lots of fruit and vegetables.

▲ Start each day with a stretch.

◀ Don't sit in front of the television or computer all day. Get out in the fresh air.

Make sure you have plenty of sleep. Children need more sleep than adults. Rest is important for your body. ▶

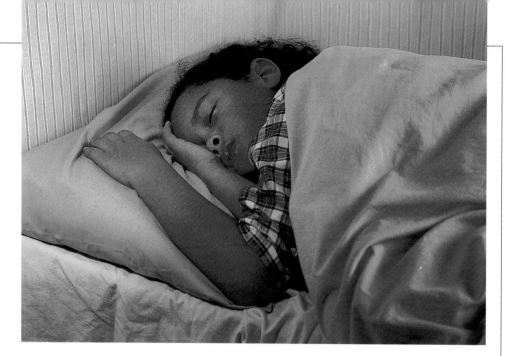

MAKE YOUR OWN PLAN TO GET FIT

1. Make a chart with a box for every day of the week.

2. Write down your favourite exercises.

3. Tick off each one, every time you exercise.

4. Try to do some exercise every day.

Exercise is fun!

It is fun to exercise with friends. Sports centres will have classes you can join. You should find lots to choose from.

You can meet new people and make friends if you play in a team.▼

You could exercise with your family and friends. It's more fun to exercise together.▼

▲ If you are on holiday you can learn new sports.
Canoeing is great fun.

Walking is good for
everyone.▼

Glossary

Asthma An illness that makes it difficult to breathe.

Diabetes A disease that makes it difficult for the body to make its own sugar.

Heart The big muscle that pumps blood around your body.

Joints The places in your body where two bones join up.

Lungs Lungs are the big muscles in your chest that help you to breathe.

Muscles Muscles make your joints and bones work, so you can move your body.

Pulse The beat you can feel on the inside of your wrist.

Skeleton The bones that make up your body.

Finding out more

BOOKS TO READ

Look After Yourself: Get Some Exercise! by Angela Royston
(Heinemann Library, 2003)

Top Sports: Gymnastics/Soccer/Martial Arts/Volleyball all by Bernie Blackall
(Heinemann Library, 1988)

The Complete Book of Bones by Claire Llewellyn
(Hodder Wayland, 2001)

ORGANIZATIONS

Health DevelopmentAgency
(this used to be called the Health Education Authority)
Holborn Gate
330 High Holborn
London WC1V 7BA
Telephone 020 7430 0850

The British Heart Foundation
14 Fitzhardinge Street
London W1H 4DH

Index